BE
MORE
SLOTH

BE MORE SLOTH

Get the hang of living life in the slow lane

ALISON DAVIES

Illustrations by Carolina Buzio

quadrille

'THE POINT OF SLOTHS
IS TO BRING A SENSE
OF WONDER, MAGIC
AND HAPPINESS TO ALL
OTHER SPECIES. DID YOU
KNOW THAT EVERY OTHER
ANIMAL'S FAVOURITE
ANIMAL IS THE SLOTH?'

Ann Burton

Slow down. Calm down. Don't worry.
Don't hurry. Trust the process.

Contents

Introduction 8

BE STILL, BE SLOTH 12
TURN THINGS UPSIDE DOWN 30
HANG IN THERE! 48
BE KIND, TO YOURSELF AND OTHERS 66
UNLEASH YOUR TALENT 84
SMILE AND FIND PEACE 102
RELEASE THE SLOTH 120

Slothary 140

INTRODUCTION

My cousin Phoebe first brought sloths to my attention. Not that I wasn't aware of these joyful creatures before, but I hadn't really studied them in any depth. On first glance they seemed cute, with their goofy features and winsome smiles, but they didn't seem to do much. How wrong could I be?

Appearances are deceptive. There's a lot going on beneath the surface of a sloth's initial sweetness. Mother Nature is a wise and mercurial being, with a reason for everything, so while these lovable and somewhat huggable creatures look like they're doing nothing, the opposite is true. They smile in the face of laziness, appearing to hang around and shoot the breeze, when really there's a biological miracle of mammoth proportions going on behind the scenes. Skilled swimmers with a vice-like grip, their talents know no end, but what's really impressive is their generous

nature. Their fur is an eco-system in its own right, providing a home and sustenance to an array of organisms. In other words, the sloth is quite literally a lifesaver, allowing a diverse collection of creatures to thrive. Some animals, humans included, might balk at this idea, but sloths understand that you can achieve so much more when you work together. And why not offer a helping hand, when all you have to do is be there and be present. Sloth world is a kind world with a sense of balance and order. 'You scratch my back, I'll let you live in my fur.' How's that for a deal? It's a blissful place where every moment is a pleasure.

I can offer you a glimpse of how the sloth works in the pages of this book, but the real insights come directly from these hairy gurus. Stare into their eyes and you'll begin to understand their true engaging nature. Take your time and enjoy as you learn the peaceful art of being. And then, and only when you're ready, you can **be more sloth!**

Be still, be

SLOTH

Be still, be sloth...

Bliss is in the cheerful, easy smile of the sloth. In that one expression you'll find everything you could ever need. Beneath those gorgeous dark berry eyes you'll glimpse dreams of the tallest trees packed to the rafters with juicy green leaves. This sanctuary is a place to hang, to rest and eat, then rest some more. Simple things matter to the sloth, and that's not because they don't have room for more complex issues in their dome-like heads. It's because they understand that everything takes time. And while we may rush through life trying to jam in as much as possible, the sloth knows that each experience takes as long as it takes and should be savoured. Why waste energy forcing matters, when you can sit back, relax and enjoy the ride?

Some of this is no doubt down to the sloth's zen-like charm, but there's also a biological reason for this *laissez-faire* existence. Sloths need to rest in order to digest! Their diet of toxic leaves wouldn't suit most, but their careful, slow digestion (around one leaf a month) allows them to absorb the nutrients while avoiding being poisoned in the process. Genius! Sloth-like ingenuity and flair should never be underestimated. They may look like they're doing nothing as they hang nonchalantly in mid-air, but that's a clever ruse. In fact, their multi-chambered stomach is working hard to break down the toxins and extract a sliver of energy, so while swift is not a word in their vocabulary, neither is slovenly.

Everything in good time, so sayeth the sloth.

Moving at 0.15 miles per hour might not float your boat, or suit the needs of a busy lifestyle, but there's something to be said for slowing the pace. It's a jungle out there, and while it may not be the tropical kind, the way of the sloth can still teach us something. When we rush, our heart rate increases, oxygen is limited, and our brain doesn't have the time or space to perform at its best. A little less haste and a more sloth-like approach allows for care and caution, two worthy bedfellows that once snuggled up provide a sense of security, power and focus. Not only that, but life becomes more meaningful. Moments that could have been missed or glossed over are enriched because we consciously engage with them. Like those luscious leaves that are not to everyone's taste, **the sloth who takes his time enjoys the sweetest nectar in the forest canopy.**

'THE TWO MOST
POWERFUL
WARRIORS ARE
PATIENCE
AND TIME.'

Leo Tolstoy

ACTIVATE SLOTH TEMPO

Imagine you could slow down time.
Make the most of every moment
and enjoy life, but still get things
done effectively and successfully.
How joyful would that be? There is a
way to 'slothify' your timetable and
do just that. No panic, no stress, no
pressure. You just need to program
your mind for the day ahead, and
let nature take its course.

1. On waking, place your feet firmly on the floor. Feel the solidness of the ground providing balance and the perfect platform for the day.

2. Breathe deeply and consider everything you want to achieve. Don't rush through this process, take your time and start with simple things like getting washed and dressed, then build up to bigger goals.

3. Imagine you're watching a film where you are the central character, the hero of the piece. See yourself achieving every single thing with ease and a big smile on your face.

4. Say: 'I digest every moment of this day, taking the time to enjoy and achieve all my targets with ease.'

5. At any point throughout the day, should you feel stressed or under pressure, breathe deeply and repeat the affirmation while picturing the smiling face of a sloth.

Be More
STILL

REST TO DIGEST
WHEN EATING.

We might not face the anguish of being poisoned by our food should we gobble it at speed, but we do face the painful prospect of indigestion. Make the most of mealtimes. Chew each mouthful mindfully and enjoy the taste and texture of your food. This brings more pleasure, helps you live in the moment, and also means you'll digest the food properly and realise when you're full.

DON'T HURRY.

You cannot hurry a sloth. You'll simply be met with a blissful expression, which works its way into your heart in seconds, mellowing all thoughts of haste. By the same token, do not be hurried in your judgements or thoughts. When something happens, resist the urge to react straight away. Instead be more sloth: take a deep breath and let yourself acclimatise to the situation.

PRACTISE THE ART OF PATIENCE.

Every day be aware of giving time to others. This could be through sharing an insight or a story to make someone smile; spending time helping someone with a chore; or giving them the space and respect they need to deal with a problem or situation.

HANG FROM OR WITH A TREE.

We may not have the super-strong or curved claws of a sloth, which make dangling from a tree look like child's play, but we can still benefit from hanging out in nature. Spend some time in the countryside or at your local park. Find a tree you like and sit beneath its boughs. Gaze up and look at the structure, the way the tree is shaped and how the branches spiral outwards. If you have an issue or problem on your mind, tell it to the tree, out loud or in your head. Then spend some time simply sitting and enjoying the company of nature. Don't rush to find a solution, just revel in the moment and let any thoughts, ideas or emotions flow through your mind.

'ADOPT THE PACE OF NATURE: HER SECRET IS PATIENCE.'

Ralph Waldo Emerson

PERFORM AN ENERGISING BELLY BREATH.

Place both hands, palm down, beneath your navel. Focus on your breathing, extending both your inward and outward breath by one count. After a few minutes you should feel a warmth emanate from your stomach. Feel this warmth fill your entire body as you breathe in, then imagine that as you exhale you're releasing this loving energy into the world. This technique helps to calm the mind and also provides an energy boost, while reminding you to think of others as you go about your day.

NEVER GET SO
BUSY MAKING A
LIVING THAT YOU
FORGET TO
MAKE A LIFE.

SLOW LIVING

- Know your priorities
- Less TV, more reading
- Less clutter, more space
- Unplug – give yourself some space from your phone
- Less focus on the future and more on the present
- Don't over commit
- Focus on single tasking

Turn things

UPSIDE

DOWN

Turn things upside down

Sloths are superheroes in furry form. They command respect. Surely not, you say. For what is a sloth if not full of sloth? Hardly the stuff of valour. Disarming, yes, and cute at best, but plucky, fearless – never! And so the sloth casts its spell, lulling the world into a false sense of security – but don't be fooled. Disarming they may be, but they're still the stuff of legend.

Take the Mapinguari, a terrifying monster at least 2m (6½ft) in height, which haunts the Amazonian rainforest. Stories abound of its ghastly appearance. With a giant, lumbering, bear-like body, it moves in a cloud of beetles and emits a foul stench. Some reports suggest

it has one eye; others say two. Most alarming of all is its mouth. Set with jagged rows of teeth, it sits firmly in its belly, ready to devour any hapless human it chances upon. While folklore is rife with tales of its grisly exploits, it's believed there is an element of truth to this creature. It comes in the shape of the giant ground-dwelling sloth: extinct for 8,000 years, this magnificent beast was bigger than an elephant. A formidable character, the giant sloth must have seemed monstrous to the ancients, who made up stories to explain its existence. And so the malevolent Mapinguari was born, a creature worthy of the finest horror tales, and with supernatural powers to boot. This sloth-like time lord had the ability to turn day into night and make those in its presence feel dizzy. It's easy to see how the giant sloth could also have created this impression. One glimpse would make the bravest warrior weak at the knees, while it's impressive stature could easily block out the sun.

But a sloth of any size has the power and might to mesmerise. Consider for a moment their long and super-strong claws, around 8–10cm (3–4in) in length. These curved beauties are used skillfully to cling on to branches with ease, and just as well, because hanging upside down doesn't come naturally to the rest of the animal kingdom. This topsy-turvy view of the world not only gives them a different perspective, it goes some way to explain their super-sloth status. Even Batman would struggle to live life this way, but the humble sloth takes it in his stride. A perfectly engineered body provides some assistance, and the special adhesions that anchor the guts to the ribs allow it to breathe, eat and even get jiggy while upturned and dangling perilously in mid-air.

Superbly simple and oh so sloth!

'IT'S USEFUL TO GO OUT OF THIS WORLD AND SEE IT FROM THE PERSPECTIVE OF ANOTHER ONE.'

Terry Pratchett

TAKE A
SLOTH'S
EYE VIEW

The key to a creative, engaging and slothful life is in the ability to look at things from a fresh perspective. Just as the sloth views the world from his upside-down vantage point, you too can embrace your inner superhero and turn things on their head. In doing so you'll see the wealth of options and opportunities available to you – no upside-down acrobatics required!

1. If you have an issue or problem, storyboard it. Draw a series of pictures with a sentence for each to describe what has happened so far.

2. When you reach the point of crisis and you're stuck – stop, breathe and take a moment.

3. When you're ready, read back through the storyboard so far, and try and look at it like a story, rather than something that is actually happening to you.

4. If it were a story, how would it end? What could happen next to resolve the situation? Draw some more boxes to tell the end of the tale.

5. Look again at what you have created. Can you think of another ending? If so, draw some more boxes to illustrate the new ending.

6. Continue to come up with as many different endings as you can. Be creative and have fun with this.

7. When you've finished, look at the story and the variety of endings. By putting the situation into a narrative format you're able to think objectively and look at it from a different perspective. This allows you to be creative and see all the options available to you.

'EVERYBODY'S
GOT A
DIFFERENT WAY
OF TELLING A
STORY – AND
HAS DIFFERENT
STORIES TO TELL.'

Keith Richards

Be More
INTENTIONAL

LIST YOUR
SUPERHERO
SKILLS.

We all have strengths and talents, but it's easy to dismiss them. Make a list of your best bits. Consider character traits like kindness, sense of humour, and so on. Also think of things you're naturally good at, like being a good cook or a great listener. If you're struggling, ask a friend or family member to help. You'll be surprised at the positive way in which others see you. Once you have your list, read it at least once a week as a reminder of your superhero qualities.

BE LIKE THE SLOTH AND MAKE THE CEILING YOUR FLOOR.

Lie down somewhere you won't be disturbed. Gaze up at the ceiling and imagine that it's the floor and you are hovering above it, looking down. It can take a few minutes to get used to the idea, but once you adjust you'll see the room in a totally different way. Changing your physical view gives you a flexible perspective and exercises the imagination, so that when you have to deal with problems you'll be able to think outside of the box.

FIND A PICTURE YOU LIKE AND KNOW WELL AND LOOK AT IT FROM A *DIFFERENT ANGLE.*

What do you see? Consider what this new angle adds or takes away from the original piece. Perhaps it reminds you of something, or stirs up conflicting emotions. Challenge yourself to look at things you know and love in new ways. You'll gain deeper insights, and your experience of the world will become richer and more vibrant.

DON'T BE AFRAID OF UNLEASHING YOUR MONSTER.

We all have a dark side, a fiery passion that sometimes verges on anger. This shadow self is not something to be feared. Instead, if we learn to acknowledge what we're feeling and why, it can help us deal with it in a positive way. The next time you feel angry or frustrated, ask yourself why and then consider what would make you feel better. Then be more sloth and channel your aggression into a physical activity, like tree climbing!

CONSIDER YOUR STOMACH AS YOUR SECOND MOUTH.

As odd as this sounds, the Mapinguari highlights an important truth. We absorb stress in many ways, and the stomach feeds on negative energy, which in turn causes a number of complaints like IBS, bloating and nausea. When you feel tense, pay particular attention to your stomach. Rub the palms of your hands together for a minute, then place them over this area. You should feel a gentle warmth beneath your fingers. Allow this warmth to spread through your body until you feel more relaxed.

LIVE LESS OUT
OF HABIT AND
MORE OUT OF
INTENT.

NEW HABITS

- Ignore nonsense
- Talk less and listen more
- Learn a new skill
- Help the less fortunate
- Laugh more
- Wake up earlier
- Lose the ego

Hang in
THERE!

Hang in there!

The sloth needs a head for heights. Living most of his life in the trees, he has little choice in the matter. If that wasn't enough of a challenge, then add in the topsy-turvy suspension and you have a physical conundrum on your hands, never mind a lethal dose of motion sickness! But let's not forget, sloths are somewhat invincible. These acrobats of the animal kingdom are built for a life in the trees. With taut yet flexible muscles, and in the case of the three-toed sloth, an extra neck vertebrae that gives them a 270-degree swivel, they work it to their advantage. Their front feet are gifted with menacing-looking claws, which allow them to hang for days, and their grip is a force to be reckoned with. Even in death it remains, held in place like cement, the sloth gives the appearance of one who has literally stepped out of the world but could re-emerge any second to enjoy the snooze it was having.

In a word, they make things look easy. More than that, *they make life look easy.* So what is their secret? Is it down to science and the way they're put together, or something altogether more mystical?

In truth, we'll never know the definitive answer. One thing we can be sure of: sloths endure. They hang in there when most would falter. They make the most of their strengths (super-strong and flexible claws) and turn their weaknesses into opportunities, hence a slow and lumbering gait on the ground means more agility when climbing trees. Life looks easy when you're a sloth, because it is. They make it so. Unlike humans who might secretly relish the stress when something goes wrong, the sloth is no drama queen. Life is made to be lived. Each day comes and goes and with it there are new challenges – a hungry jaguar, a lack of leaf fodder, depleted energy levels – but the sloth gets on with it.

No mess, no fuss, just a calm, balanced and tenacious attitude.

'PATIENCE AND
TENACITY ARE
WORTH MORE
THAN TWICE
THEIR WEIGHT OF
CLEVERNESS.'

Thomas Huxley

SLOTH AND STEADY WINS THE RACE

The winner of the race isn't always the one that comes first. Rushing through life, we miss so much, and we don't always perform at our best. Over time, all the frenzied activity and stress takes its toll, leaving us lost, with all sense of purpose gone. To prevail and prosper, take a steady yet determined approach and you'll find life, and all its challenges, flow with ease.

1. Stand with your feet wide apart.

2. Drop your weight into your knees, in a lunging position.

3. Bounce up and down and feel the weight in your thighs. Notice how your legs support you; like the trunk of a tree they provide balance.

4. Now straighten your legs and reach up with both hands, so that you're pointing upwards and slowly stretching your spine.

5. Imagine you're suspended from the branch of a tree. Recognise that your body is flexible, it allows you to do the things you need to do, like hanging in there when you need to, and also moving with ease.

6. Bring your arms down to your sides. Breathe deeply and say in a loud voice, 'I am a dynamic force. I move through life easily and always reach the right destination.'

'THE TRUEST WISDOM
IS A RESOLUTE
DETERMINATION.'

Napoleon Bonaparte

Be more

DETERMINED

IF AT FIRST YOU DON'T SUCCEED, CLIMB HIGHER.

If you have a specific target or goal in mind, think of a symbol that sums up what this means to you. For example, if you're looking for career success, you might picture a gold star, or if you're hoping to pass your driving test, you might see a car. Next, visualise a tree in your mind. At the very top of the branches sits your symbol; all you have to do is climb to the top. Imagine climbing the tree, reaching the top and collecting your prize. To finish, draw a picture of the tree with your symbol. Stick this somewhere you'll see it every day, to remind you to hang in there, keep climbing and striving!

PRACTISE TENACITY.

Every morning and evening, look in the mirror
and say, 'My tenacious spirit keeps my grip firm
and my focus clear.' Repeat ten times while
making tight fists with both hands. Get louder
and more confident with every repetition.
During the day, remind yourself of your
tenacious spirit by gripping both fists.

HANG AND ENJOY
THE MOMENT.

When you're aiming for success, remember
to enjoy the journey. Appreciate those small
victories, just as a sloth would appreciate the
view of the forest canopy or a luscious crisp
leaf on which to nibble. It's important to stop
and give yourself some credit for the things you
have achieved so far. If you're struggling, enlist
a friend or family member to remind you
of your accomplishments.

GIVE YOURSELF HEIGHT AND S P A C E.

You might not feel agile enough to scale a tall tree, but you can still bring height into the equation by climbing a hill or mountain, or going to the very top of a tall building and taking in the view. Breathe deeply and take note of the vista. Let the sense of space soothe your body, mind and soul.

MAKE YOUR WEAKNESSES YOUR STRENGTHS.

Draw a line down the centre of a piece of paper so that you have two columns. In one column list the things you consider to be your weaknesses. So you might say, 'I can't run fast,' or 'I'm not good with words.' In the column next to each weakness, think of a positive way to use this, so you might say, 'Instead of running, I take my time and appreciate the scenery,' or 'I use my artistic skills to sketch pictures in my mind and on paper to help me describe things.' Get into the habit of turning negatives into positives and you'll find life becomes more enjoyable.

YOU CAN DO ANYTHING BUT NOT EVERYTHING.

BE KIND TO YOURSELF.

- Your mistakes are part of your learning
- Accept your weaknesses
- There is no right way
- Stand up for what you believe in
- Don't compare yourself with others
- Surround yourself with people who want you to succeed
- Don't underestimate your talents

Be kind, to
yourself and
OTHERS

Be kind,
to yourself and others

Kindness is the sloth's ethos. Sloths realise the benefit of working together with others, of lending a helping hand (or in the sloth's case a patch of fur). These friendly creatures are a walking ecosystem. They provide shelter and sustenance to a specific type of moth that lives in their fleece. If that wasn't enough, they also play host to algae that grow in the grooves between their hairs. While this might not sound an attractive prospect (the algae render them an itchy forest green), to the sloth who takes everything in its shambling gait it's a small price to pay. Even the presence of hundreds of moths, which dive from their fur during grooming sessions, is not a problem for this chilled-out fur ball. Instead they use their enormous claws carefully, so that the moths can track their movements and anticipate a lunging hook, thus avoiding a savage skewering.

This gentle benevolence is repaid in a number of ways. The camouflage that the algae provide is essential in the sloth's survival, and this is just as well for it has many predators. This is another good reason for taking refuge in the treetops, and while two-toed sloths might make the most of it, the three-toed variety have something of the James Bond about them. They like to dice with death at least once a month, when they come down from the safety of the branches to defecate on the forest floor.

This daredevil escapade may seem foolish at first glance, but delve a little deeper and the ingenuity of the sloth is revealed. The dung it deposits is a gift to the pregnant moths within its fur. They lay their eggs in the excrement, and then the caterpillars feed on it. Once fully mature, they fly up into the trees and make a cosy home in the sloth's fur, where they live out their days. Nitrogen is produced as they decompose, and this is what the camouflage algae (which are also a supplementary food source for the sloths) need to grow. And so the cycle goes on, and the sloth wins every time. This walking food factory synthesises its own sustenance. As far as science goes, that's beyond advanced!

Of course, it's impossible to tell the sloth's true feelings about its fluttery tenants. Whether they're messy, loud and unreasonable is anyone's guess. The sloth appreciates that each species has something to offer, a talent or strength that might differ from their own, but which is still of great value. Slow on the surface they may be, but sloths are ahead of their time. They recognise the power of diversity, kindness and working together to not only survive, but thrive with style and grace; something we as humans could benefit from in our busy lives.

'NO ACT OF
KINDNESS, NO
MATTER HOW
SMALL, IS EVER
WASTED.'

Aesop

OPEN YOUR HEART, SLOTH STYLE

It's easy to care for those who mean something to you and who are on the same wavelength, much harder to cultivate affection for those you don't know and who think differently. The sloth manages to look after its guests with ease, creating a workable relationship which nurtures all involved. Practise opening your heart by activating the energy centre known as the heart chakra.

1. Place both hands over the centre of your chest and imagine you're cupping a ball of orange light.

2. Feel the light getting bigger and brighter. You should notice heat emanating from your palms and filling your chest.

3. Notice the warmth spreading throughout your body.

4. Picture a stream of bright orange light pouring from your heart chakra. This loving energy helps you to connect with others in a positive way.

5. Smile, and know that, like the sloth, you have an open and giving heart.

Be More
THOUGHTFUL

DEAL IN THE CURRENCY OF KINDNESS.

Do one thing every day for someone else. Offer your time, a kind word, some encouragement, or simply lend a hand. The more kindness you share, the more you'll receive, so make it a part of your daily routine.

APPRECIATE YOUR DIFFERENCES AND LEARN FROM THEM.

In life, you're not going to get on with everyone. There will always be a person who rubs you up the wrong way and gets under your skin. While this is not literal, as in the fur of a sloth, it can still feel suffocating and have a negative effect on your well-being. When this happens, sit for a moment and meditate. Think of all the things that irritate you about this individual. Take each quality that you don't like and consider if you have it too. We are often drawn to people, good and bad, because we share similar qualities, so if someone annoys you because they are impatient, then think about your own behaviour and if you share this trait. If you do, think of ways that you can change this for the better. Our outer world, including the people in our life, is often a reflection of who we are, so when we behave in a loving way we attract loving people and vice versa.

PAY *attention* TO OTHERS.

Notice how they look, how they sound, and listen to what they're saying to you. We often cruise through life not really hearing other people. This lack of attention causes misunderstandings, and acts as a barrier to communication. Instead, make a point of asking questions and ensuring those nearest and dearest, and also those you know less well, are genuinely okay. When we listen to others we learn and appreciate so much more.

GIVE YOURSELF A HUG.

You might not have the super-flexible arms of a sloth, but you can still give yourself a metaphorical cuddle by acknowledging all of your lovely traits. Treat yourself as you would a friend, and big up your achievements. Say, 'I am doing well!' several times until you truly believe it, then imagine a giant pair of furry arms enveloping you in a cuddle.
How nice is that?

CARRY A PIECE OF
ROSE QUARTZ.

This beautiful pink crystal is thought to heal the heart and amplify loving energy. Wear or carry a piece and you'll radiate love wherever you go. There's no guarantee it will bring you new romance or your own mobile ecosystem, but you will look and feel gorgeous, particularly if you wear this pretty stone around your neck.

'KINDNESS IS THE LANGUAGE WHICH THE DEAF CAN HEAR AND THE BLIND CAN SEE.'

Mark Twain

SLOW
PROGRESS IS
BETTER THAN NO
PROGRESS.

10 STEPS
FOR SUCCESS

- Try
- Try again
- Try once more
- Try it a little differently
- Try it again tomorrow
- Try and ask for help
- Try and find someone who's done it
- Try to determine what isn't working
- Try to determine what is working
- Just keep trying

Unleash your
TALENT

Unleash your talent

We can't be good at everything. Even the sloth recognises this fact. A creature of innumerable talents, yes, the unassuming sloth plays to his strengths. After all, what could be sweeter than the tender twinkle of those glossy dark eyes, or that beaming face as it lights up the Amazon? We're talking top-notch red carpet cuteness with a capital C! And we already know about this animal's super-strength steely claws and head for heights. But it's also true that while it might take the tips of the starry forest sky by storm, the adorable sloth is a little less sophisticated when it hits the ground. 'Awkward' and 'unwieldy' are two words which spring to mind, made worse by its sluggish footfall. As always, the sloth is quick to realise that walking isn't part of its repertoire, and while a stumbling step can be somewhat endearing, it can also prove fatal if you end up careering into the jaws of a ravenous jaguar. So what does it do? It unleashes yet another hidden talent.

The sloth swims, and it doesn't need armbands!

Moving three times faster than it does on land, it cuts a fine, streamlined figure. And while it might not have mastered the front crawl, it has learnt that a speedy doggy paddle approach coupled with a touch of breaststroke will get it from A to B in no time. It's unlikely there'll be any prizes for flair and dexterity, but then sloths don't go much for synchronised swimming. To them, the ability to stay afloat and advance with power and strength is all that matters. That, and the fact that it's fun!

Ever practical, the sloth has one more string to his bow. He can slow his heart rate down to such a pace that it's possible to hold his breath for around 40 minutes under water. Crucial for those life-and-death-moments when you need to escape the clutches of a predator, or if you're just trying to take a bath in peace.

It might seem that whatever the sloth turns those long-clawed paws to is a triumph, but the truth is it uses its skill set. Unlike humans who like to bemoan their weaknesses, sloths prefer to focus on what works, what they're good at, and, most importantly, what they enjoy – and you can't argue with that.

'EVERYBODY HAS TALENT,
IT'S JUST A MATTER OF
MOVING AROUND UNTIL
YOU'VE DISCOVERED
WHAT IT IS.'

George Lucas

DISCOVER YOUR SLOTH STRENGTH

Some people know instantly what they're good at, while for others the process of unearthing true talent takes time. As any sloth worth his fleece will tell you, it takes as long as it takes. Tap into your inner sloth strength and you'll feel calm, grounded and ready to walk the path of self-discovery.

1. Close your eyes and concentrate on your breathing.

2. As you breathe in, imagine you're drawing the air up from the earth, through each foot, along your legs and body, and finally into your head.

3. As you exhale, imagine the breath escaping through the top of your head.

4. Slow your breathing down as you do this by counting out a beat in your head. Then extend both your inward and outward breath by one count.

5. Imagine that each 'in' breath draws strength and energy from the earth, and each 'out' breath releases any tension you may be feeling.

6. Repeat this exercise for a couple of minutes every day and you'll feel instantly calmer and ready to engage with the day.

Be More
POSITIVE

DO WHAT YOU ENJOY.

It makes sense that the things we love doing are the things we become good at. Even if you aren't a natural ballroom dancer, or your artwork is hardly a masterpiece, the fact that it gives you pleasure is the most important thing. When we're having fun we're engaging our creative spirit, and this gives us a new lease of life and a more positive way of being. Make a list of all the things you love doing, and make sure you do at least one of those things every week. Be sure to alternate between different activities too!

BECOME A
WATER BABY.

Like the sloth, you can easily find your feet and
your way in the world when you're submerged
in water. Stand in the shower and let it cascade
over you. Close your eyes and imagine you're
bathed in cleansing light. Each spray of water
is washing you clean of any negative thoughts
or stresses that have been holding you back.
Emerge feeling refreshed and invigorated,
ready to unleash your hidden talents on
the world!

DON'T FIXATE ON
THE NEGATIVES.

Instead of concentrating on the things you cannot do, be like the sloth and focus on the things that come naturally. At the end of every day, acknowledge everything you've done well in a journal. Little things count, so anything from making a tasty and nutritious meal to fixing that wonky shelf should be included. By the end of the week you'll have lots of items noted. Reading through the journal will help you identify where your skills and talents lie.

LEARN TO ACCEPT COMPLIMENTS.

Giving compliments is one thing, but taking them can be a different matter. Don't hide your light; let it shine, and enjoy the praise that others give you. Talents are there to be recognised, so be like the sloth, flash your sweetest smile and accept that others love you!

BOOST
YOUR CONFIDENCE.

Think of a time when you achieved something, or felt happy and confident in your own skin. This could be a moment from childhood or something more recent. Relive the memory, bringing to mind all the positive emotions you experienced. As you do this, press the thumb and index finger of your right hand together firmly. Whenever you need a confidence boost, or just a reminder of your brilliance, bring your thumb and finger together in the same way to trigger those joyful emotions.

LET YOUR SMILE
CHANGE THE
WORLD BUT DON'T
LET THE WORLD
CHANGE YOUR
SMILE.

**THE LITTLE
THINGS IN LIFE ARE
WHERE WE FIND
REAL, TRUE JOY.**

CONSIDER OTHERS

- Put yourself in other people's shoes
- Open the door for others
- Give someone special an unexpected gift for no reason
- Don't interrupt or talk over others
- Apologise when you mess up
- Be patient
- Do a favour and expect nothing in return
- Consider the 'bigger picture'
- Make a small gesture of kindness
- If someone is sad try to cheer them up
- Keep things positive
- Smile more

Smile and FIND PEACE

Smile and find peace

Sloths smile all the time, every day.

While this is likely because of their facial colouring and their curious-shaped mouths, there is also much for them to smile about. These gentle creatures are Zen with a capital Z. You only have to watch a sloth sleeping, curled in the crook of a tree, to see that they are totally at peace with the world. What's more, they're at peace with themselves and happy in their own company. Sloths don't need to surround themselves with noise and confusion to feel like they belong. From their lofty treetop vantage point, they are free to breathe and appreciate the joy of living. As humans we have a tendency to clutter up our lives with material stuff, losing ourselves in the high-pressured whirl of social media, but superficial concerns mean little to the sloth. These savvy creatures are content going solo, preferring the space to contemplate such matters as their next snoozing position. That said, the connections they do make are meaningful and filled with love. The sloth baby spends several weeks clinging to the belly of its mum, and even when it finds its feet (or claws), it stays by her side for up to four years. This bond secures the animal's future, providing a strong foundation from which it can flourish.

Sloths may not advocate large social groups, but they do understand the importance of nurturing their loved ones and themselves. While we might consider an afternoon nap a tad indulgent, to the sloth it's a necessary part of their routine. Fancy some time out at the gym, perhaps a dip in the pool or a luxurious spa treatment? The sloth says yes, as she plunges head-first into the sparkling depths of a tropical stream, or inhales the sweet headiness of the forest fauna. But while her leafy home might emit a pungent scent, the sloth herself is odourless. With only 25 per cent muscle mass, this lady doesn't even glow, never mind perspire in the enduring heat. It's a clever tactic which keeps her safely hidden from predators. Some say, because of this lack of scent, that those who encounter a sloth smell what they want to smell, projecting their own thoughts, emotions and imagined scent upon the creature. Easy to believe when you consider the charming nature of the sloth. One glance at its comical but perfectly formed features could melt the hardest heart, transporting it back to memories of childhood pleasures.

So what lessons can we learn from this? We live in a world where things must get done, but how we do them is very much up to us. Taking a more leisurely approach works in some cases, but even if your life demands action, it's essential to find those moments of peace, those times when you can be yourself and be happy. Start with your breath, then move on to a sloth smile and feel it sweep through body and soul. For your finale, work in some time to do your own thing, then finish with a resounding moment of silence and just be.

'PEACE BEGINS WITH A SMILE.'

Mother Teresa

PRACTISE SMILING LIKE A SLOTH

Sloths radiate happiness. They do this naturally. We can do the same, and in doing so will attract a wealth of good fortune and joy. This is because the positive energy we give out acts like a magnet, drawing more of the same happy vibes in our direction. Practise this technique daily and, like the enigmatic sloth, you'll feel altogether more joyful and content with your lot.

1. Find a quiet spot where you won't be disturbed. Make sure it's a comfortable space where you can sit.

2. Burn some geranium essential oil, or add a few drops to a bowl of hot water and inhale the gentle aroma. Geranium is an uplifting scent known to balance the emotions.

3. Place your hands either side of you, palms pressed against the floor to anchor your body as you breathe deeply.

4. As you exhale, smile and imagine the warmth emanating from your eyes, filling the space around you. Think of something you love as you do this, and it will increase the flow and strength of these feelings.

5. Let your smile get bigger and brighter with every breath.

6. Picture the space you're sitting in flooded with a pink gooey substance. See it extending outwards to fill the room.

7. Take this a step further and imagine the pink goo seeping through the walls, spreading outside and spilling over into the streets until it bathes everyone and everything in the rosy, gloopy glow of happiness.

'THE LIFE OF INNER PEACE,
BEING HARMONIOUS AND
WITHOUT STRESS, IS
THE EASIEST TYPE OF
EXISTENCE.'

Norman Vincent Peale

Be More
CALM

MAKE SOME
S P A C E.

Can't see the wood for the trees? Let the sloth
be your guide. Declutter your life by clearing
some space. Start with physical things, taking
it room by room. Be honest and ask yourself
what you no longer need, or haven't used/
worn in over a year. By making room physically,
you'll feel less stressed and be able to breathe
in your environment; this relieves emotional
pressure and allows you to think clearly. When
you're ready you can move on to decluttering
your life in other ways. Take each area – work/
relationships/health – and consider who or what
brings you joy, and also what brings you down.
Once you've identified this, you'll know what to
avoid and where to find your peace.

SMILE, OFTEN.

Like the sloth, make this your default expression. You'll feel better, even if you have to force it; the facial movement tricks the subconscious mind into believing you really do have something to smile about. What's more, smiling is contagious. Once you start you can't stop, and those on the receiving end also pick up on the vibe. Soon everyone you encounter wears the same cheesy grin. If you need further inspiration, take two minutes to browse some sloth pics on the internet. You'll be beaming from ear to ear within seconds.

SLEEP WHENEVER YOU FEEL THE NEED.

Don't feel guilty for nodding off. It's your body's way of telling you that you need to rest. Consider the sloth. His body is a temple. He knows that for every action, there is a reaction. For every movement or physical function, energy is required. If that energy is depleted then the body doesn't work as it should. Food is undigested, movement non-existent, and the clever cycle of life that the sloth has built begins to crumble. We also need energy to carry out daily tasks. If we're constantly running on empty, our health suffers. Give yourself a break, and get the rest you deserve. Consider it as important as exercise and make it routine.

GO WITH THE *flow*.

Allow yourself to live in the moment. This means stopping every once in a while to look around. Just as the sloth admires the view from his treetop palace, you need to appreciate your surroundings. Practise taking five minutes out of your day, just to focus on what you can see, hear, smell, touch and taste. Ask yourself, 'What am I feeling right now?' Try not to change this or force anything, just let the feeling take its natural course and learn to become a spectator in your own life. Practising this skill will help you deal with stress in an effective way, because you'll find it easier to detach from a situation and view it objectively.

HUG THERAPY.

Sloths like to cuddle, and with their enormously long arms they're more than equipped for the task. A hug is a shorthand version of a cuddle, with the same warmth, energy of feeling and healing benefits. Try and give at least one hug a day, and never limit your hugs. Reaching out to others in this way is good for the soul. It boosts oxytocin, known as the 'cuddle hormone', so that both you and the hug-ee reap the rewards. And as clever sloths know, it's almost impossible to give a hug without getting one in return!

'NATURE DOES NOT HURRY YET EVERYTHING IS ACCOMPLISHED.'

Lao Tzu

GET CREATIVE

- Stop trying to force it. Take a break and do something different.
- Ease yourself in with some carefree, playful creation.
- Create what you WANT to create, not what you think you SHOULD.
- Go for a walk to get some fresh air.
- Get your heart pounding with some exercise.
- Be inspired by the work of other creatives.
- Make sure you're getting enough sleep.
- Have a go at a creative skill you've never tried before.
- Set yourself a challenge against the clock.
- Acknowledge that you aren't perfect, but creative anyway!

Release the
SLOTH!

Release the sloth!

Sloths may be slow, oozing like treacle from a spoon as they creep through the trees, but quiet? Not likely! While they move like furry assassins melting into the jungle backdrop, they like to be heard in a variety of ways. The sloth has a voice, and it knows how to use it. It's hard to imagine such a docile and magnanimous creature making a racket, but never let it be said that the sloth is predictable. This animal knows exactly how to express itself and has a sound for every occasion.

Get under its ecosystem of a skin and you'll hear a hiss worthy of the feistiest viper. It starts small, the gentle deflation of a balloon, and escalates depending on the level of annoyance. When in distress the canny sloth emits a low, bleating call, which to other sloth ears able to detect low-frequency sounds is enough to let them know what's what. Squeals

and grunts are also part of its repertoire, and baby sloths love nothing more than a good squeak – although this is not an excuse to squeeze one! Should an errant scamp find themselves far from the reach of Mum's long arms, they'll emit a tiny bleat, which is sure to have her moving turtle-like to the rescue.

Speaking of the female of the species, lady sloths are sassy with a capital S. They know exactly what they want and how to get it. Surreptitious flirting in the form of coy glances is not their style. Confidence has never been an issue for these girls. They're a tad more proactive, screaming at full pelt to alert any likely lad in the vicinity that they're ready and available for love. This loud screech may seem ungainly, but it does the trick, so much so that sloth suitors come in their droves and often have to fight each other for the privilege of a first date. To us, this no-nonsense approach may lack romance, but the sloth ladies' outspoken charm makes them irresistible to their own kind. Their ability to express themselves clearly, and with the self-assurance of one who is happy with who and what they are, is key.

It's hard to imagine a creature more comfortable with its lot. Content to be themselves in every way, joyful for each breath, and able to assert their wishes with confidence, clarity and their own unique voice, the sloth has life sussed, and so can you if you follow their lead. Instead of hiding your light in the bushes, be bold and proud of who you are and what you have to say.

Release the sloth and speak your inner truth, then watch as the world falls gracefully at your feet.

'LOGIC WILL GET
YOU FROM A TO B.
IMAGINATION
WILL TAKE YOU
EVERYWHERE.'

Albert Einstein

RELEASE THE SLOTH!

While hanging from a tree and screeching at full throttle might not appeal to you, there's still a way to release your inner sloth and tap into the power of your unique voice. Performing a series of simple stretches and emulating this mighty creature will help you express yourself and restore oomph. Practise this exercise daily, if possible, and you'll notice over a period of a few weeks that you'll feel more confident, eloquent and able to speak your mind.

1. Find a quiet place where you won't be disturbed, and you can do your own thing without feeling in any way embarrassed.

2. Stand with feet hip-width apart, shoulders relaxed.

3. Close your eyes and focus on your breathing. Notice the gentle sound it makes and how your chest moves. Pay attention to the rhythm and slow each breath down.

4. From the waist, gradually roll forwards so that you are looking at your knees. Let your arms hang loose and continue to breathe deeply.

5. Put yourself in the position of the sloth. Imagine you're in the rainforest hanging casually upside down from a tree. What does it feel like? Can you feel the stretch along the backs of your legs and down your spine? Pay attention to each muscle and how it feels. Continue to breathe steadily.

6. Clasp the backs of your calves and, if you can, bring your head to your knees in a further gentle stretch.

7. Slowly unfurl from this position until you're back where you started.

8. Take a deep breath in, then shout the first word that springs to mind. It doesn't matter what it is or how silly it sounds. The point is that you express what you're feeling, right now, in the moment. Put some energy into this, and shout as loudly and often as you like.

'THE ONE THING THAT YOU
HAVE THAT NOBODY ELSE
HAS IS YOU. YOUR VOICE,
YOUR MIND, YOUR STORY,
YOUR VISION. SO WRITE
AND DRAW AND BUILD AND
PLAY AND DANCE AND LIVE
AS ONLY YOU CAN.'

Neil Gaiman

Be More YOU

TURQUOISE IS A STONE ASSOCIATED WITH SELF-EXPRESSION AND CREATIVITY.

The colour stimulates the flow of energy, particularly around the throat area, so wearing a turquoise scarf or necklace made from the stone can help you find the confidence to speak your mind. Alternatively, picture a ball of turquoise light hovering over your throat. As you breathe in, the warm energy of the light seeps under your skin, relaxing your neck muscles. As you breathe out, any worries or fears related to speaking your mind are released. Repeat this breathing technique for a couple of minutes, then to finish say, as loud as you can, 'I am sloth. Hear my voice!'

GET WITH LIKE-MINDED SLOTH BUDDIES AND FORM A STORYTELLING CIRCLE.

Make a point of meeting on a regular basis and sharing your tales. These can be stories from personal experience or tales you've heard, read, or even made up. Flex your imagination and give each session a theme, for example 'fairytales' or 'funny stories'. As the weeks progress, you'll find your creativity soars, and you'll be bubbling with new ideas, thoughts and opinions.

GET SHARING.

Get into the habit of sharing how you feel with one person every week. This could be sharing a joy, an experience or a challenge you've faced, or telling them how you feel about them. You might want to share or relive a specific memory. As you open yourself up to communication, you'll find that others will also communicate more effectively with you and the bonds that tie you together will get stronger.

Sing

AT THE TOP OF
YOUR VOICE.

Imagine, like those loved-up sloth ladies, that you want to attract some attention. Put on your favourite song, something upbeat and powerful, and picture yourself under the spotlight. Imagine you're performing it to an audience and feel their adoring eyes upon you as you belt out the lyrics. The more you throw yourself into the tune, the more applause you receive. You're the star and everyone wants to hear you sing. Enjoy the moment, then whenever you're in a situation where you feel nervous or afraid to express yourself, recall the tune and the memory of taking centre stage to create a sense of confidence.

WRITE IT DOWN.

Sloths may not have mastered the art of the written word, but they know the importance of getting things off their chest and out in the open. When someone upsets you it's not always easy to let them know. This could be because the moment has passed, or you don't want to hurt them, but it means that the feelings fester, causing further upset. Instead of letting this happen, tell them how you feel in a letter. Write from the heart and pour your emotions into every word. When you're done, light a candle and burn the letter in the flame as a way of releasing your thoughts.

SLOW DOWN AND
TRULY SEE THE
THINGS THAT
MATTER MOST.

FIND YOUR PASSION

- Pay attention to each moment of your life – begin paying attention to what is happening in your life, notice where you are and practise being fully present.

- Pay attention to how you feel – let yourself feel things. This will guide you to discover what you truly love and are passionate about.

- Put yourself forward – stop thinking about what others are thinking. Put yourself first and prioritise what you like and want to do.

- Take pride in your talents and accomplishments – spend time on you. Get to know yourself, what you love and listen to what your heart wants to do.

- Write it all down and reflect – note down your favourite experiences and life lessons so you don't forget them. Keep track of your thoughts and actions so you remember the most important moments of your life.

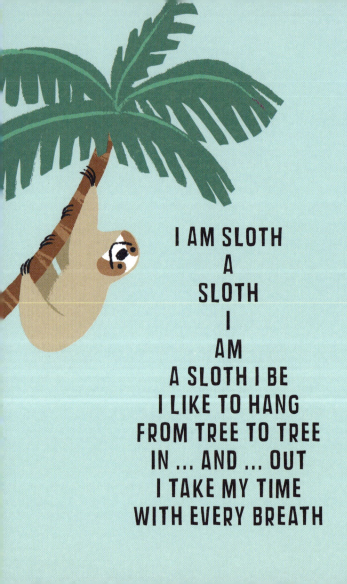

I AM SLOTH
A
SLOTH
I
AM
A SLOTH I BE
I LIKE TO HANG
FROM TREE TO TREE
IN ... AND ... OUT
I TAKE MY TIME
WITH EVERY BREATH

ANOTHER RHYME
AND LIFE GOES BY
IN SUCH A WHOOSH!
YET STILL I HANG
THERE
IS
NO
RUSH
I'VE FOUND MY PLACE
AND THIS IS ME.
A SIMPLE SLOTH
I LIKE TO BE ...

SLOTHARY

#hangingout: Dangling from branches is the only way to be seen.

#livelittlethings: It's all about those small pleasures in life.

#slothlove: When you love sloths so much that you get stuck in a sloth-based internet spiral.

#slowliving: Know your priorities.

Ballroom dancer: Something a sloth will never be.

Belly breath: Filling your tummy up with air until it resembles the glorious potbelly of the voluptuous sloth.

Climbing: If you don't climb you won't shine.

Cuddles: An extended hug. Also acceptable in the form of squeezes and snuggles.

Determination: Keen to munch on some delicious poisonous leaves? Let no one stand in your way!

Doggy paddle: The optimum stroke of the bathing sloth.

Hairy gurus: Aka SLOTHS.

Haste: The opposite of sloth tempo.

Head for heights: As S Club used to say: reach for the stars! Just beware of the motion sickness.

Heart chakra: The source of all positive sloth energy.

Hugs: A shortened cuddle and favourite sloth pastime.

Internet: Google. Baby. Sloths. Now.

James Bond: Dicing with death, experts in camouflage – it's time the sloth was made an honorary Double-O.

Kindness: The sloth's ethos – flash that smile furry friends!

Mapinguari: With supernatural powers and jagged teeth this creature is the stuff of nightmares (… or dreams if you're a sloth lover).

Moths: Roommates of the sloth. Though their fluttering may get annoying at times they're really co-dependant besties.

Nonchalance: Say BUH-BYE to anxiety and fuss.

Oomph: Fill yourself with this to experience ultimate sloth euphoria.

Oxytocin: The cuddle hormone. Spread the love.

Plucky: Do not underestimate the sloth.

Positivity: Should just be called slothitivity.

Rose quartz: The stone of lurrrve. Keep a piece on you at all times to radiate happiness.

Sloth baby: The cutest damn thing you will ever see.

Sloth tempo: A very, very slow speed … think school disco slow dance.

Slothify: Channel the sloth 24/7.

Sluggish: Next time someone calls you out for being lazy just tell them you're energy efficient.

Snoozing: NEVER feel guilty for napping.

Synchronised swimming: The sloths' favourite spectator sport.

Tenacity: Being clingy is okay when you've got super-strong claws looking for abundant branches.

The Amazon: A favourite sloth hangout.

Topsy-turvy: Upside down/head over heels/bottom up. The wrong way up is the new cool. See *Stranger Things* for reference.

The Tortoise and the Hare: The sloths' fave fable.

Tree climbing: Ditch the gym and make for the forest.

Trees: Sloth homes.

Turquoise: The stone of energy!

Water baby: Mermaids eat your heart out – the sloth is pool perfection.

Winsome smile: The cheesy expression plastered on every sloth face.

Publishing Director Sarah Lavelle
Editor Harriet Butt
Editorial Assistant Harriet Webster
Designer Gemma Hayden
Illustrator Carolina Buzio
Production Director Vincent Smith
Production Controller Jessica Otway

Published in 2018 by Quadrille,
an imprint of Hardie Grant Publishing

Quadrille
52–54 Southwark Street
London SE1 1UN
quadrille.com

Cataloguing in Publication Data: a catalogue
record for this book is available from the
British Library.

Reprinted in 2018
10 9 8 7 6 5 4 3 2

ISBN 978 1 78713 227 6

Printed in China